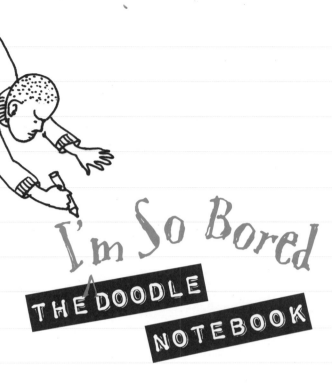

I'm So Bored

A THE DOODLE

NOTEBOOK

Written & Illustrated by

Susan McBride

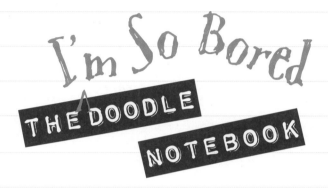

I'm So Bored

THE A DOODLE NOTEBOOK

Written & Illustrated by
Susan McBride

LARK BOOKS

A Division of Sterling Publishing Co., Inc.
New York

Editor: Joe Rhatigan
Art Director: Susan McBride
Assistant Art Directors:
Shannon Yokeley
Bradley Norris
God of the Scanner: Jeff Hamilton
Art Intern: Ardyce E. Alspach

Library of Congress Cataloging-in-Publication Data

McBride, Susan (Susan A.), 1962-
  The I'm-so-bored doodle notebook / written & illustrated by
Susan
McBride.-- 1st ed.
       p. cm.
  Includes bibliographical references and index.
  ISBN 1-57990-767-9 (hardcover)
 1. Doodles. 2. Drawing--Technique. I. Title.
NC915.D6M385 2006
741.2--dc22

2005033976

10 9 8 7 6 5 4 3 2 1

First Edition

Published by Lark Books, A Division of
Sterling Publishing Co., Inc.
387 Park Avenue South, New York, N.Y. 10016

© 2006, Lark Books

Distributed in Canada by Sterling Publishing,
c/o Canadian Manda Group, 165 Dufferin Street
Toronto, Ontario, Canada M6K 3H6

Distributed in the United Kingdom by GMC Distribution Services,
Castle Place, 166 High Street, Lewes, East Sussex,
England BN7 1XU

Distributed in Australia by Capricorn Link (Australia) Pty Ltd.,
P.O. Box 704, Windsor, NSW 2756 Australia

If you have questions or comments about this book,
please contact:
Lark Books
67 Broadway
Asheville, NC 28801
(828) 253-0467

Manufactured in China

ISBN 13: 978-1-57990-767-9
ISBN 10: 1-57990-767-9

For information about custom editions, special sales, premium
and corporate purchases, please contact Sterling Special Sales
Department at 800-805-5489 or specialsales sterlingpub.com.

Dedicated to
Annie, me, and the cherry tree.

Introduction

Being bored is boring. Maybe you're bored right now. In fact, perhaps it was your utter boredom that compelled you to pick up this unassuming guide. If so, consider yourself lucky, because this book is actually an authentic anti-boredom device. Cleverly disguised as a mild-mannered classroom notebook, The I'M-SO-BORED DOODLE NOTEBOOK is a license to doodle anytime, anywhere. It's a place where it's okay to let your mind wander and your creativity to take over. Whether your boredom stems from you being a product of the industrialized world* or you're on a tedious trip with your family, OR you're sitting in school learning about common denominators, this book will help you dump the doldrums and banish boredom.

Boredom devils BEGONE!

Not only is there lots of space inside to doodle your day away, but you'll have the opportunity to "knit" a sweater for an octopus, create a kudzilla monster, negotiate the three stomachs of a cow,

* Before the big, dirty, grinding Industrial Revolution, the word "boredom" apparently didn't really exist. The "feeling" was called many other things like "ennui," "malaise," even "NOONDAY DEMONS." (Kinda poetic for something so persistent and unpleasant, huh?)

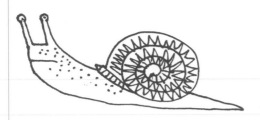

create your rock band's logo (even if you don't have a rock band), kick up your dream wheels with fantastic bodywork, and way, way more demented doodling fun.

About to get caught by a prowling teacher or mad parent? No worries. Simply flip to the real fake notes in the center of the book and look studious. This should scare off the non-doodle friendly adults in your life.

So, get the lead out, sharpen that pencil, and fight the good fight! Write and doodle all over this book. Copy my doodles. Create your own. Ignore my simple directions and do whatever you want. (Hey, it's your book now.)

TEMPORARY RELIEF FROM BOREDOM may be achieved by reading and doodling in this notebook (use as directed).

You're bald!

You're BLAH

SIGH***

In your battle against boredom, you will need a weapon.

The trusty pencil, great for smudging and shading.

The crayon, time-honored and waxy!

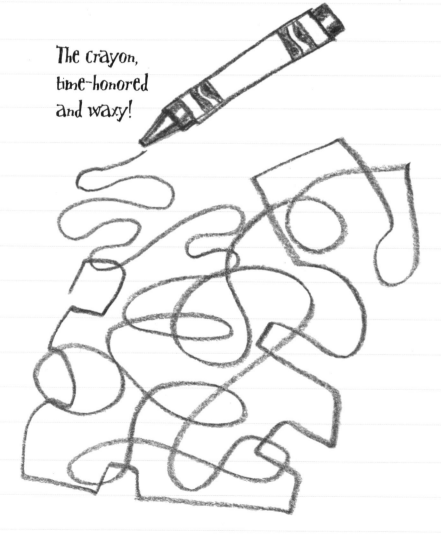

OK, as mentioned, you're bored—

Here's an opportunity to escape. How are you going to DO-ODLE it?

Dig out?
Spiral staircase?
Ladder?
Airlift?
King Kong?
Draw your escape now!

It's up to you.

Be creative when finding your way.

Myths from ancient Greece feature the maze as a symbol for life's trials and tribulations.

Those underpants are not flattering.

Who asked you?

Let's Fight!

Hideous half-man, half-bull MINOTAUR MONSTER

You are here!

Labyrinths have a continuous
path: there are no dead-ends
as with mazes. Go ahead—
try it out.

Draw your own maze or labyrinth ... it's not as easy as it looks.

THE godS
MAJOR & MINOR DEITIES
ANCIENT TIMES

People once thought that floods, tornadoes, plagues, and bounty were all provided by the gods. The mood of the gods had a lot to do with this, and that included boredom. Being the plaything of a moody god is risky business—it might take an ice age to lodge an unhappy god or goddess out of a bad mood.

"Cupid, take aim at that short fellow; let's get this party started."

People in positions of power (over YOU!) can take themselves a little too seriously ...

Bored* of Education (*get it?)

EXTREME MAKEOVER!
Doodling to the rescue!
(AN ASSESMENT)

Update this hairstyle.

Dude, yer BALD. Trade the comb-over for a soul patch.

New glasses, perhaps?

Spiff up the suit; add pizazz.

Start with a SMILE.

Good raw material, but shift the attitude!

Leave loud plaids for the guys with the bagpipes.

See? A little doodling made all the difference.
(A SOLUTION)

The no longer BORING Board of Education

A few simple swipes of the pen and you've got different expressions on the same mug. Observe.

The look of BOREDOM is achieved by making spaced-out eyeballs and little lines under the eyes. The mouth is a straight line.

HEAD INJURIES can be indicated by an enlarged pupil in one eye. The curvy eyebrows add a splash of anxiety.

ANTICIPATING PAIN (like a snowball to the back of the head) is easy. Pinprick eyes, a frown, and raised eyebrows do the trick.

HYPNOSIS or TELEVISION WATCHING is similar to boredom. Add swirls in the eyes for that special vacant stare.

Give it shot, and try it yourself.

Add a body?

Ah ... the Family Meeting
—prime time for major boredom.
What would spice up this little gathering?

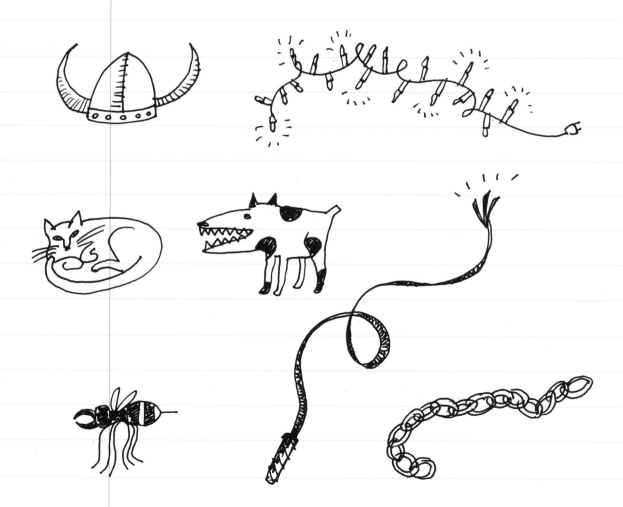

Perhaps Dad would look good in a Viking hat with horns?
Grandma's walker would look great with twinkle lights.
Mom could use a boa ... keep going.

TV is highly
overrated.

All 300 channels.

Look, Pumpkin, rigor mortise is starting to set in!

Cool, when will he be ready for eating?

ps. Never trust a cat.

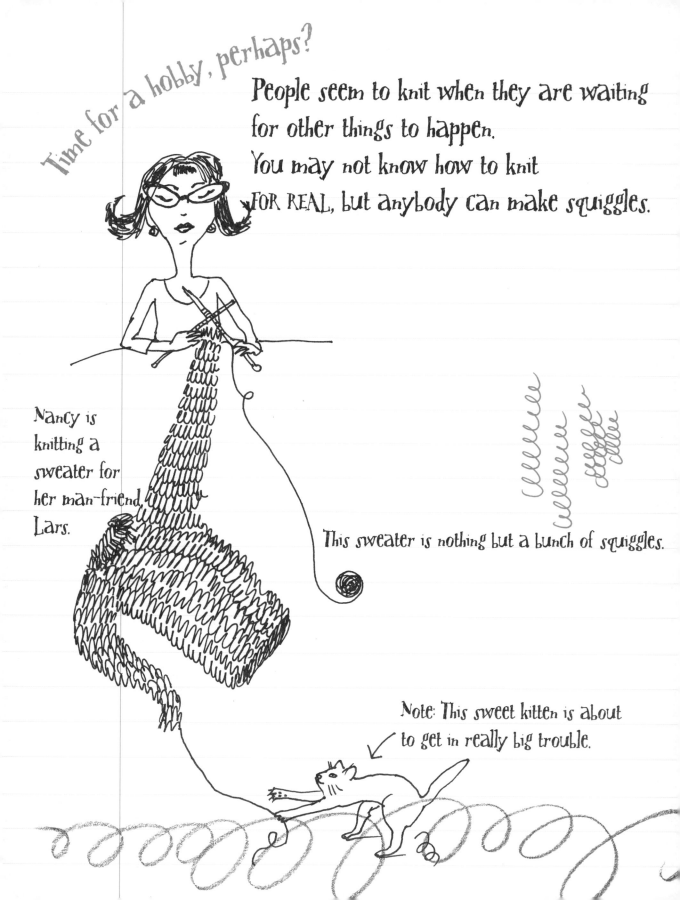

Time for a hobby, perhaps?

People seem to knit when they are waiting for other things to happen.
You may not know how to knit FOR REAL, but anybody can make squiggles.

Nancy is knitting a sweater for her man-friend Lars.

This sweater is nothing but a bunch of squiggles.

Note: This sweet kitten is about to get in really big trouble.

Give it a go—make squiggles.

Help Lars finish knitting his dog, Aldo, a sweater.

What is Ya Ya knitting?
Help her finish.

"I am a deeply superficial person."

ANDY WARHOL

ARTIST & FILMMAKER
1928-1987

Andy was an oddball. He
wore a weird white wig
and slouched a lot. His
most famous paintings
are of mass-produced
products like cans of
soup and familiar
portraits of well-
known celebrities.
The assembly-line
quality of his
work seems to
comment on the
modern, mundane
backdrop of our
busy, little media-
fueled lives.

sigh

So you don't like your options?

Why not stand things on their heads?

Get surreal!

A while back a bunch of artists, who called themselves Dada-ists and SURREALISTS (I'm not making this up) grew weary of looking at pretty landscapes and portraits of idle rich people ... so they shook things up a bit.

To come up with new ideas for creating art and literature, they played doodling and writing games.

The non-boring activities on the next page may interest you as well.

The ultimate doodle:

Automatic Drawing

This is easy. Take a deep breath, open your mind, and put the pencil to the paper. Do not lift it—draw what's in your head— anything that comes to mind.

Try it, and don't censor yourself! Go with the flow.

Automatic Writing

requires three or more people. Are there three or more bored people in the vicinity? (Here's one now). ⟶

The surrealists were into this thing called "collective creativity" ... which means they liked to steal ideas from each other. You can do this too and maybe laugh out loud while you are at it. Here's how.

1 Take a deep breath, open your mind (yeah, yeah), and write down one sentence on a piece of paper. It can be a question or a statement.

2 Allow the person next to you to read your sentence. He will then add his own sentence below yours.

3 Before passing the paper to the next person, the second player folds the paper over the original sentence—hiding it from the next player. The third player will add a sentence under the second player's sentence, fold over the paper, and pass it to the next person, and so on.

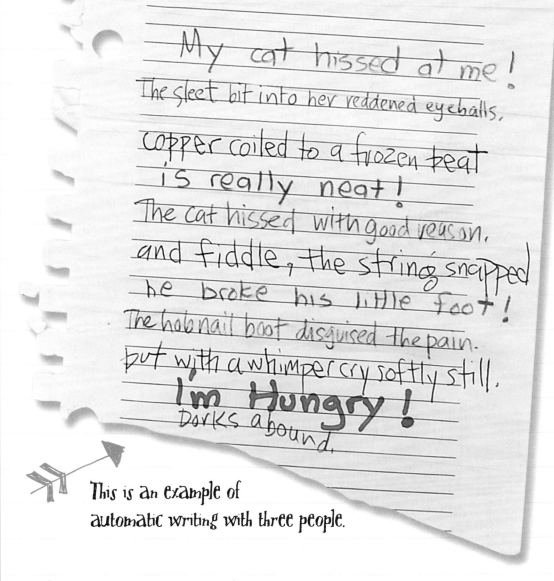

My cat hissed at me!
The sleet bit into her reddened eyeballs.

Copper coiled to a frozen teat
is really neat!
The cat hissed with good reason.
and fiddle, the string snapped
he broke his little foot!
The hobnail boot disguised the pain.
but with a whimper cry softly still.
I'm Hungry!
Dorks abound.

This is an example of
automatic writing with three people.

4 When the paper is all used up, the most pompous person in the
group unfolds the whole thing and reads the "poem" aloud.

Creative work done collectively,
or in a group,
is often called

Exquisite
Corpse!

Viva la doodle!

Stunning!

EXQUISITE CORPSE games can be played like automatic writing. You can fold a piece of paper, do your thing, and hand it off to the next person. You could also work on it all at once, like this.

Create your own collective piece of anti-boring art.

NOT! **HISTORICALLY** **BORED**

"People go to great extremes to accomplish very little."

RUBE GOLDBERG

CARTOONIST & SCULPTOR

1884-1970

Rube was a mechanically inclined kinda guy. He studied engineering, but spent most of his life doodling and cartooning. He was pretty good at it, too, and even won a Pulitzer Prize (which is way cooler than an Oscar or a Grammy). He is most famous for inventing complex machines that ultimately performed very simple tasks. Now that you know about him, you will hear his name used in reference to all kinds of complicated and absurd situations.

Having trouble getting up in the morning? ⟶

Take a page from Uncle Rube's book. Create a machine to make your life SEEMINGLY easier.

What kind of Rube Goldberg device can you devise?

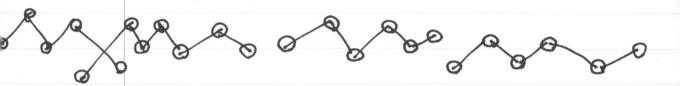

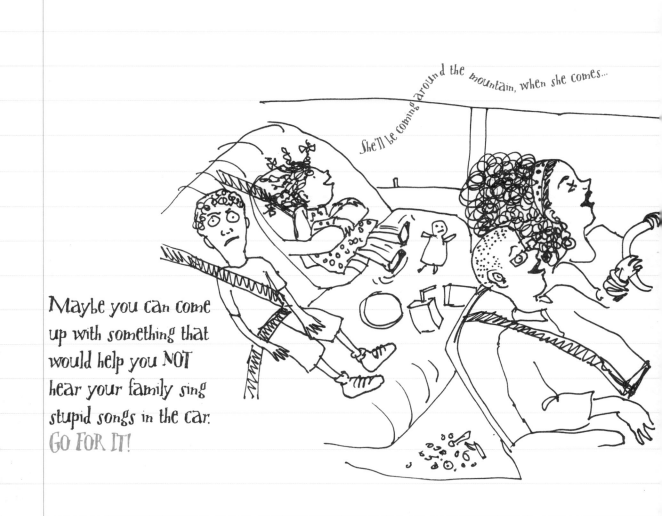

Maybe you can come up with something that would help you NOT hear your family sing stupid songs in the car. GO FOR IT!

41

PASATIEMPOS GALLO, S.A.

LA ROSA

"I want to be left alone."

GRETA GARBO
FILM STAR
1905-1990

An eye roller and heavy sigher, this beautiful Swedish actress had it all—fame and fortune. After making many successful films, Greta had had it. She chucked it all, turned her back on all those noisy, clamoring fans, and lived a very quiet life indeed—ALONE.

Add pupils.

EYE ROLLING
(similar to boccie ball)

The next time you get a lecture about ROLLING YOUR EYES, try this. Tell the pontificating parent that eye rolling is actually a form of EXERCISE, practiced by yogis and other really together, spiritual people.

Let me know how that works out for you.

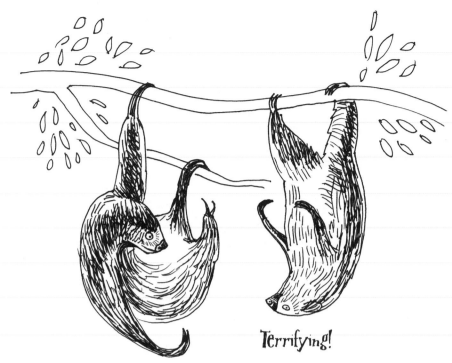

Terrifying!

What a nightmare!
I dreamt that I was
exercising!

What a BOAR!

Some people think that boredom and its good-for-nothing friend, sloth, are the ROOT of all EVIL!

What would an evil plant look like? DRAW one here: ——→ Would it have thorns? drip blood? hideous blossoms? poison berries?

What we have here class, is the root of all evil!

Check it out: a boring bug.

Draw an evil garden
while you're at it.

Pssst! Fake Notes
on the next page!

Georgraphy + History
Class notes 3/14

Europe, 6th largest continent, has (46)
countries. Technically not a continent, But part
of pennisula of Euroasia (including
Europe & Asia.)
Separated from Asia by Russia's Ural Mts
in the East, & the Caspian Sea +
Black Sea in the south east.

Highest point is Mt. Elbrus in in
European Russia at 18,481 ft. (5,633 m)
North of Georgia/ Russian border
Stuff like this on exam.

Explore (5) themes
× Land masses, geography
× Ethnic conflicts
× Population Explosion, Famine, Pestilence
× Governments
× New Europe — Global community

① Geography

* Land masses, Bodies of Water

In Europe:

North Atlantic Ocean
Norwegian Sea
Irish Sea
Celtic Sea
Bristol Channel
English Channel
Bay of Biscay
[Baleanic Sea
  Ligurian Sea
  Gulf of Venice
  Adriatic Sea
  Mediterranian Sea
[Tyrrhenian Sea
  Ionian Sea
  Sea of Crete
  Aegean Sea

* At least
  10 on exam-
must be able to
locate on blank
map. See map
in book & on
worksheets in

Mr. B's office.

There are definitely EVIL PLANTS. Invasive vines can take over gardens and choke the life out of them. One in particular has become known as the plant that ate the American South!

KUDZU!

Pronounced cud-zoo.

A BRIEF HISTORY

Fragrant!

Kudzu was given as a gift from the Japanese people to the Americans in 1876. It was considered exotic and beautiful.

Miraculous!

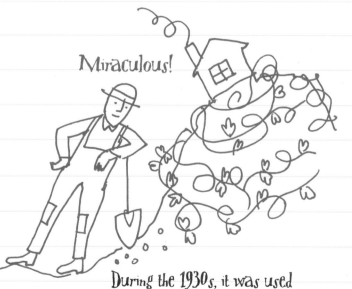

During the 1930s, it was used to help control erosion, with great effect.

Mommy!

In the 1970s, kudzu was declared a WEED and a scourge! It had consumed entire farms and pulled down forests. People have been trying to kill it ever since.

Like so many things, it starts off so innocently.

In the wrong climate, kudzu can grow up to one foot a day.

Figure 1. A streetlight

OK, there is one cool thing about kudzu. It creates terrifying topiary ...

KUDZILLA!

Come closer, I wish to ensconce you!

Figure 2. A streetlight transformed into KUDZILLA!

Transform this quiet scene
into a kudzu drama by
doodling your own
KUDZILLA!

gracious.

"Let them eat cake."

MARIE ANTOINETTE
QUEEN to
LOUIS XVI OF FRANCE
1755-1793

Poor Marie just wasn't that bright. Known as a giggler and yawner at court, she is purported to have suggested that the starving peasants of her country eat cake when told they had no bread. Telling hungry people with pitchforks and a new-fangled guillotine to eat cake is truly dumb. She lost her head—her life cut short by lack of interest in important matters.

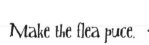

Make the flea puce.

Puce

Pronounced py-oos.
A deep-red to dark
purple color. French for, "FLEA."
EW.

C'est la vie!

bonjour

A French Lesson (in Dullness)

whoop tee dooo

Ennui
Pronounced an-wee.
Noun. Listlessness,
general dissatisfaction,
lack of interest.

Use ENNUI in a sentence.

i.e.: The French class abated its ennui by lobbing
crêpes Suzette at one another.

Taupe

Pronounced tope.
A brownish-gray color.
French for mole—a small,
brownish-gray rodent.

Use TAUPE in a sentence.

i.e.: The taupe dress hung on the woman's skeletal frame, emphasizing her pallor.

Oooh la la, what are you looking at?

Make the dress taupe.

mercy!

I spy something poofy.

Poodle Do-odles!

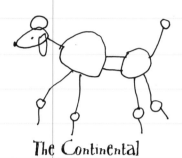

The Continental

The English Saddle

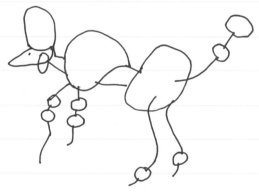

The Jiggy Do

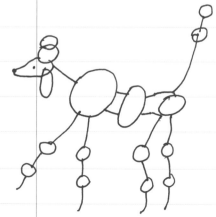

The Pompous Pompadour

The Ice Cube

People tend to think of Poodles as French dogs—
OH, but NO, er Nein! They are of German origin.
They were called "puddle" dogs (puddle-poodle)
and worked as retrievers for hunters.

NUDE poodles!

Quick, poodle doodle a dog-do and help these naked beasts regain their decency!

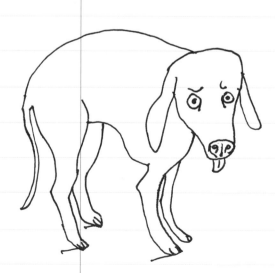

I don't know about
you, but I kinda like
being naked.

Add curls.

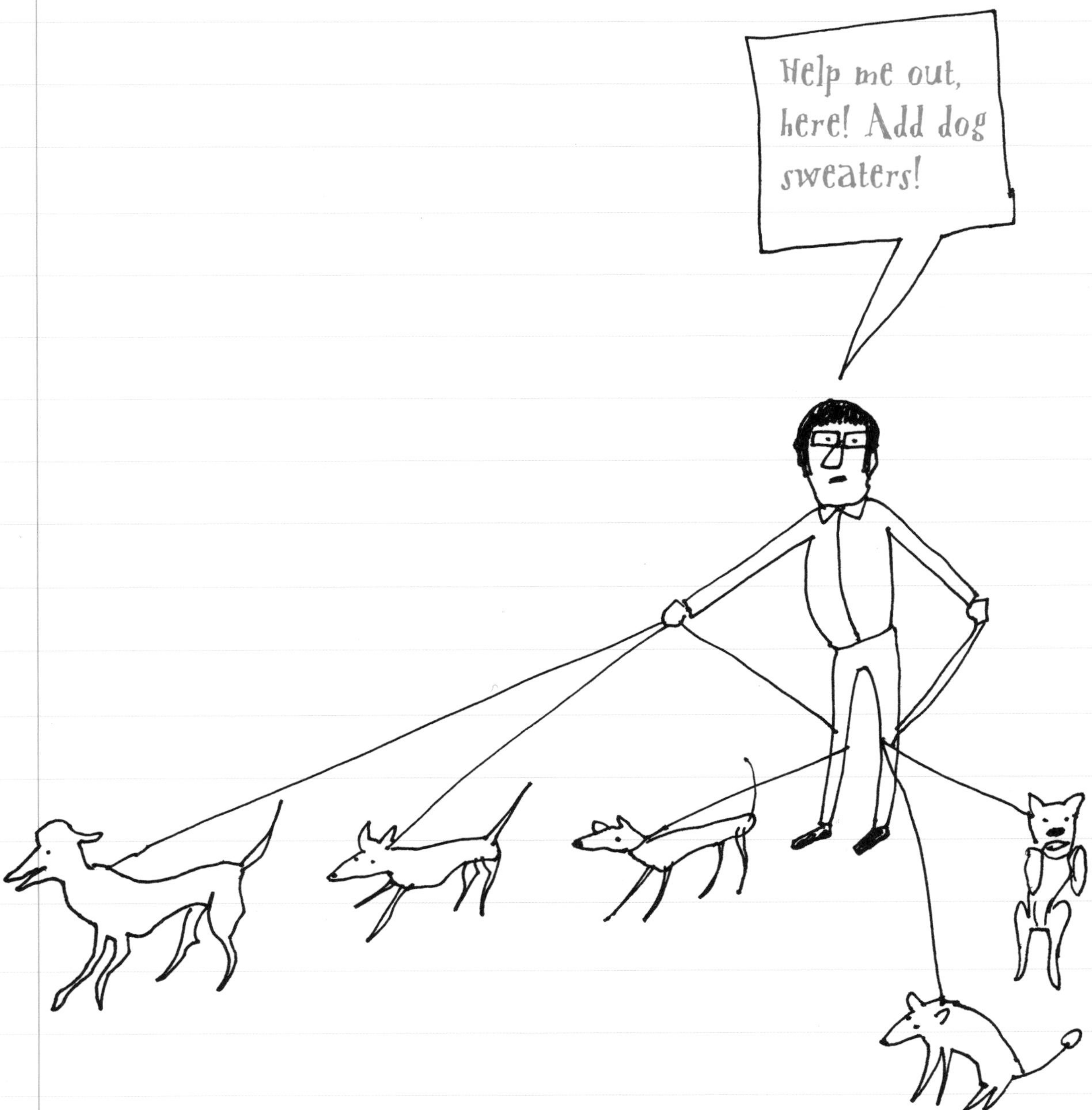
Help me out, here! Add dog sweaters!

IGGY POP

GODFATHER of
PUNK ROCK
1947-

Iggy began
life as James
Osterberg, Jr. in the
Midwest of the United
States. He's been mak-
ing loud music and
complaining of bore-
dom since he was in
high school. His
style has influenced
countless punk bands
the world over, even
though he has never
had a top 10 album
himself. Said to have
invented the STAGE
DIVE, Iggy continues
to rock and roll.

"I'm the chairman of the bored."

Have you ever considered starting a band?

Adoring fans would be just one benefit. You could also hang out with friends in your uncle's garage and annoy his neighbors—now that's not boring.

Sound check, check, check, check

What would you name your
band if you had one?

Bad Tuna
Slicked Back Ninnies
Pixel Dixy
Glitta Sistas
Random Crud
Tedious Trudy
Myopic Visions
The Mistakes
Digital Doo Da
Piercing Eardrum
Overproduced Null
Trumped-up Foo
Pantsuit Situation
Dandy Dingbat
Moot Pointe
Overwrought
Torpor
Sashimi Sundae
Dead Horse
Sleeping Dogs

keep going ...

Your band
logo here.

What kind of music
would YOU perform?

Create a wardrobe for these musical divas.
Doodle something up for them, and make it snappy!

Poof with the
attitude!

Pixel Dixie (and president of the 1-H Club):
sings his new hit single,
" Big Hair Girl"

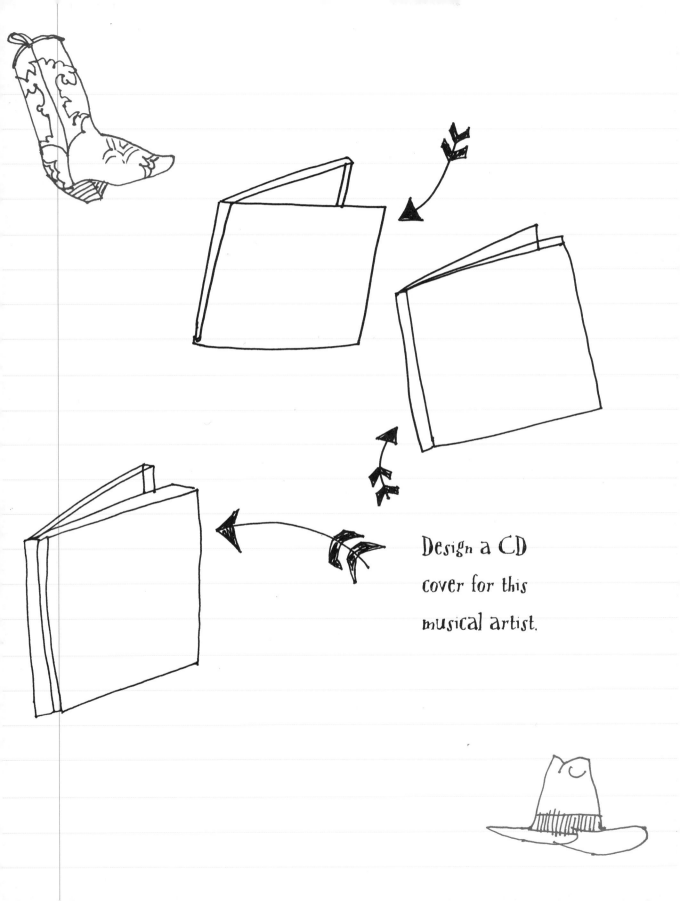

Design a CD
cover for this
musical artist.

If you get real famous, you'll need bodyguards.

Help this dude get into the groove.

yo yo yo

Add some chunky jewelry.

Okay, so now you're famous and even have a groupie! Sadly, you might find all the attention and autograph signing a tad tedious ...

How are you going to escape? You'll need some wheels.

Put a shimmy in your front end!*

Personalize your ride!

Don't be idle, even if you don't yet drive. Emblazon the wheels that express your style.

Carlito's Body Shoppe

* TRANSLATION: To put a shimmy in one's front end roughly means to enhance the performance of a motor vehicle: either through engine work which would enable the vehicle to accelerate faster or possibly to emit exhuast with a prounounced and desired sound. Also, one could decorate said vehicle in a conspicuous manner.

"Ladies and gentlemen, choose a motif!"

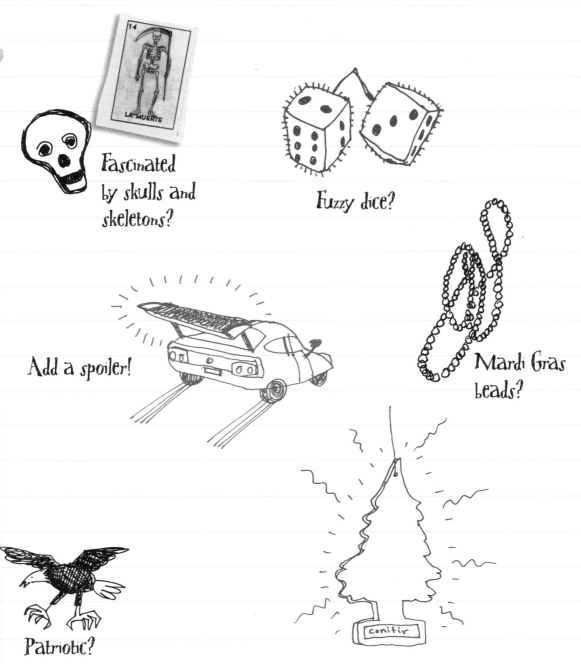

14
LA MUERTE

Fascinated by skulls and skeletons?

Fuzzy dice?

Add a spoiler!

Mardi Gras beads?

Patriotic?

Cat pee problem? Replace it with pine fresh scent!

conifir

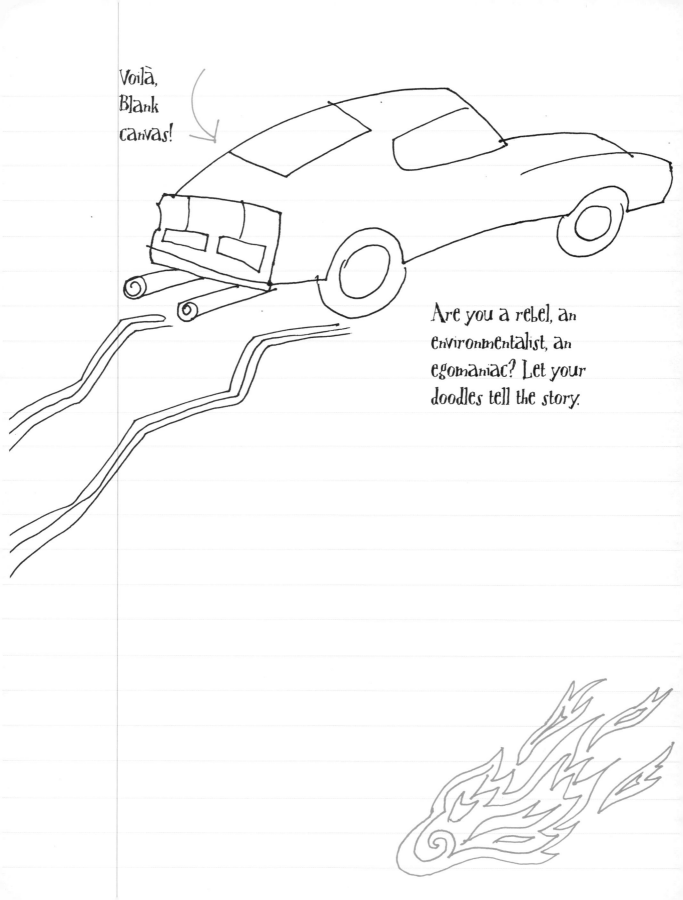

Voilà, Blank canvas!

Are you a rebel, an environmentalist, an egomaniac? Let your doodles tell the story.

Draw yourself behind
the wheel. Add flames to
the hood, perhaps.

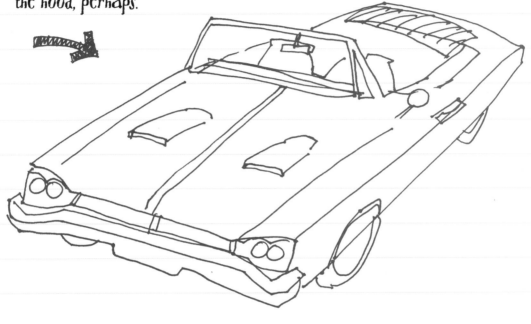

Don't forget the wheels!

Have glue gun, will travel.

Amber made an ART car by gluing 3,243 artificial flowers onto her mom's car.

Way to go, Amber!

Make your own art car.

My endless summer vacation ...

"When I look back on my Childhood, it seems quite gloomy."

ANTON CHEKHOV

RUSSIAN WRITER,
DRAMATIST & PHYSICIAN
1860-1904

It seems Russian people know something about boredom—all the ice and snow may have something to do with it. Anton Pavlovich Chekhov was a great observer of human behavior. He wrote a renowned short story called <u>The Dreary Man</u>. But he is most famous for his plays, one of which was called <u>The Seagull</u>. He often wrote about people who were bored beyond belief and expecting the worst.

What does boredom look like?

Draw in a face of moody self-absorption.

Do you ever get the impression that

Yes, dear.

your parents might be more bored than you?

Have a nice day, dear.

Question: What is more dull than listening to other people's cell phone conversations?

Watching

paint

dry?

WRITE CAPTIONS
(For some of the most insipid "communication" on planet earth!)

Idle Hands, Idle Minds

Sometimes it seems bored people like to make a big deal out of nothing, just for a little (pathetic) excitement. You'd never do this, would you?

Figure 2. Molehill

Figure 1. Mountain

There's another way to say making a big deal out of nothing:

tempest in a teacup.

Storms represent creativity, so go ahead and doodle some up.

What kinds of storms are
brewing in your teacups?

An Alberta Clipper
A squall
A nor'easter
A typhoon
A tsunami
Drizzle
Sleet
A hurricane
Snow
Freezing rain

... It's up to you.

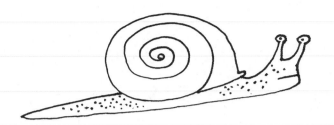

Muses are typically beautiful, magical women who appear out of the mist and help you come up with ingenious ideas.

Okay, so boredom doesn't exactly fit the typical muse profile. But she can help you get things done.

And she's always available.

Fellow doodler, I leave you with these
words of wisdom.

"The cure for boredom is curiosity.
There is no cure for curiosity."

—Dorothy Parker

(attributed)

Well, that's just great!

Acknowledgments

I'm fortunate to work with a great group of people at Lark Books. Special thanks to Joe and Celia for continued enthusiasm and help with this project. Thanks to Nicole for coming up with the title. Cheers to Bradley, whose computer bombed every time he tried to scan artwork for this book. Thank you Jeff for your patience and for tales of your troubled cat, Myra. Megan and Kristi, it was fun making surrealist poetry with you for this book.

Accomplished doodlers, Michael and Peep, life would be dry as dust without you. Nathan, Bella, and Luna—I'm terribly fond of you.

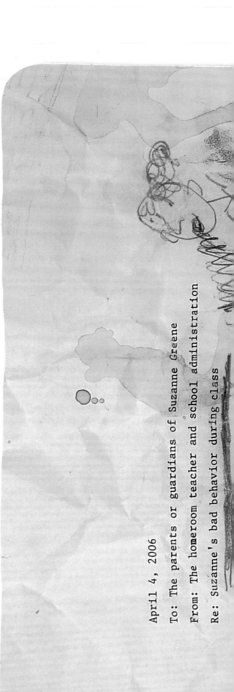

April 4, 2006

To: The parents or guardians of Suzanne Greene

From: The homeroom teacher and school administration

Re: Suzanne's bad behavior during class